DIVORCE

OVER

CORNED BEEF

AND CABBAGE

GO FROM A MARITAL MESS TO A MARRIAGE THAT'S BLESSED!

BY: RICHARD & RENDA HORNE

Take note that the name satan and associated names are not capitalized. We choose not to acknowledge him, even to the point of violating grammatical rules.

ISBN 0-9769831-5-x

Business Builders Writing Services (BBWS)
P.O. Box 1493
Buford, Georgia

Printed in the United States of America

DEDICATION

This book is dedicated to our children, and children's children. We hope that you guys will humbly submit yourselves to God, always cleave to and trust His word, walk in His wisdom, and resist all demonic provocations, and execute 100% FAITH activation. We release the Blessing upon you to grow forward!

WE THANK YOU...

Lord & Savior Jesus Christ:
You are the Savior of our souls, and the foundation of our marriage and family. There are no words in any earthly language that can truly describe our love and appreciation for You, all You have done, all You are doing, and all You will do, in, and through our lives. There is undoubtedly none like You. You deserve all the glory, honor, and praise…thank You!

Our Children & grandchildren:
You all are the priceless loves of our life. We thank God so much for you guys, and love you more than you know.

Our Parents
Richard Horne Sr, (Sharon Horne – deceased), and Teola Funches – we thank you for all you have done. Your love, encouragement, and support mean so much to us. We are honored to be your children. We thank God for, and appreciate you guys more than you know!

Family & Friends:

We thank you and appreciate your encouragement and support. We love you all.

Apostle Jose & Pastor Keila De La Rosa:

We love, thank, and appreciate you two.

Apostle Lennell & Dr. Carol Caldwell:

Thank you for your blessed leadership, instruction, impartation, and awesome example of marital success.

Special Thanks:

Pastor Eric Powell – Thank you for your obeying God, and allowing yourself to be the vehicle in which He used to speak His plan into our lives almost two decades ago. We appreciate and love you – Big Brother!

Don't Divorce Over Corned Beef & Cabbage

TABLE OF CONTENTS

INTRO

CH. 1   FINDING HIS RIB & RECEIVNG HER RACK   21

CH. 2   LIVING & LOVING STRATEGICALLY   31

CH. 3   RESTORING THE LENSES OF LOVE   41

CH. 4   DON'T DIVORCE OVER CORNED BEEF & CABBAGE   55

CH. 5   THE POWER OF AN INFLUENTIAL MAN   71

CH. 6   THE POWER OF AN INFLUENTIAL WOMAN   85

CH. 7   HOW TO GET YOUR "LIKE" BACK   103

CH. 8   BECOMING A POWER PAIR   121

INTRO

"But 'God made them male and female' from the beginning of creation. 'This explains why a man leaves his father and mother and is joined to his wife, and the two are united into one'. Since they are no longer two but one, let no man split apart what God has joined together."

(Mark 10:6-9 NLT)

I f you were asked if you believe that there is a large number of broken marriages in the United States, how would you answer? How about if you were to take a survey of random people and ask them if they believe there is an overwhelming number of broken marriages plaguing this country? Would you agree that chances are the majority, including yourself, would answer yes? Whether young or old, rich or poor, religious or atheist, educated or illiterate, black, white or otherwise, it is highly likely majority would answer with a firm and absolute yes. We too use to think similarly – that is until we discovered the truth.

Let us begin first by dispelling the myth that there is an existence of *broken marriages*. Neither the United States, nor any other country on this earth has ever had, nor ever will have the problem of broken marriages. Although some statistics show that the divorce rate in the church is equal to, or possibly higher than those outside of the church, we strongly disagree. Let us be perfectly clear in stating – we firmly believe there is no such existence of broken marriages of any kind. We can only imagine what you must be thinking right now, "***These two must be crazy!***" Believe it or not, it is the truth, the whole truth, and nothing but the truth as you too will soon learn as you read on.

Both husbands and wives undoubtedly face challenges and pressures collectively, as well as individually. At times, this can be a breeding ground for bad decision making. Yet, the "bad" decisions they make as individuals or as a couple does not redefine "marriage" itself as bad or broken – and rightfully so. God created the foundation of marriage strong and unbreakable. The bible states in Genesis 2:24 that because Eve herself was literally formed out of one of Adam's ribs, presented to Adam by God, and united with the "rest-of-his-rack;" the two (husband and wife) become "**one-unit**" in the flesh. So, in order for a married couple to actually separate from one another to become "two" separate individuals, the "<u>one</u>" unit would have to be broken – not the institution of marriage itself.

For example, take sex for instance. God created sex incorruptibly pure and pleasurable within the sanctity of marriage, as well as the way in which mankind reproduce. When people choose to misuse it by acting upon impious and misguided sexual desires, it is their thoughts and actions that are bad or corrupt – not sex itself. Their actions do not negate the foundational intent for it, and therefore cannot redefine sex as "bad" or "broken." Therefore, we can take solace in the fact that God created marriage perfect and unbreakable, and contrary to popular belief it remains as such.

Unfortunately, too many people have accepted the lie (originated from satan) that the institution of marriage has the capability of being broken or redefined. However, it is individuals themselves, the husband and wife, who are susceptible and vulnerable to brokenness. In reality, there is an existence of <u>two</u> <u>fallible</u> <u>individuals</u> who together enter into the <u>infallible</u> covenant of marriage. So, although broken marriages do not exist – broken people do.

Although not all, many divorces are a result of mentally, physically, emotionally, or sexually wounded and broken individuals, who enter into the covenant of marriage unaware of his or her condition or its severity. Most often their wounds are deeply imbedded, but appear to be sustainable. One's wounds may stem from traumatic experiences such as rejection, a disability, a lack or deficiency or basic resources, insecurity, a genetic dysfunction, family (substance, mental, sexual, or child) abuse, betrayal, prolonged anger, bitterness, resentment, or unforgiveness. As a result, hurt people tend to unintentionally, as well as intentionally, hurt other people when they fail to get the wisdom and understanding that leads to his or her deliverance and healing.

(Make no mistake, we in no way, shape, or form excuse violence of any kind. No man, woman, or child should be on the giving or receiving end of domestic violence or assault. That kind of behavior should not be accepted or tolerated.)

The root of these serious issues may be deeply submerged within a person; hidden, quieted, and unrevealed prior to marriage. Still, they can be dramatically expressed during the most minute opportunities, adding a severe strain on a marriage and family. Please understand…we can definitely relate! Many years ago, our marriage was in a similar, if not worse state. In fact, it got so bad, that we almost divorced over corned beef and cabbage. It's true! We seriously almost ended our marriage, destroyed our family, and aborted God's purpose and plan for our lives over something as trivial as corned beef and cabbage.

The bible refers to the marriage relationship as "**the vineyard of love**" and recognize these "corned-beef-and-cabbage" like situations as "**little foxes**," and warns couples to "***Catch all the foxes, those little foxes, before they ruin the vineyard of love***" (**Song of Solomon 2:15 NLT**). In fact, satan will strategically plant "little foxes" all around the perimeter of a couple's marriage or "*vineyard of love*" like bombs in a mine field! His plan is to lure a husband or wife out of the safety and sanctity of the marriage covenant, in hopes of having a front row seat as he watches that husband or wife self-destruct by way of distraction, disobedience, deception, detachment, pride, and rebellion.

ILLUSTRATION:

One makes a _conscience decision_ to step outside of his or her marriage covenant, and he or she enters into adultery (distraction and disobedience.) Because it appears that nothing "bad" happened the first, second, or maybe even tenth time, he or she establishes a false sense of security (deception and detachment.) One of the enemy's most effective strategies, especially when it comes to adultery, is for a person to believe the false perception that one is so smart, in one's own wisdom, that he or she can operate "incognito" for as long as one chooses and enjoy the best of both worlds. The enemy loves it when a person believes the lie that his or her deceptive strategy is foolproof; and as a result, he or she refuses to change (pride and rebellion.) Still, this unequivocally is a deceptive lie!

God's Word confirms:

> ➢ _"For all that is secret will eventually be brought into the open, and everything that is concealed_

will be brought to light and made known to all."
(Luke 8:17 NLT)

➤ *"It is He who reveals the profound and hidden things; He knows what is in the darkness, and the light dwells with Him."* (Daniel 2:22 AMP)

It is extremely important to operate in obedience and God's wisdom and not to venture outside of your *marital vineyard.* Doing so will help you avoid demonic traps, and consequences that can blow you to bits!

When it came to our own marriage years ago, the truth is, our major blow up over "*corned beef and cabbage*" was only a fraction of all the shattered pieces or "*little foxes*" of our brokenness as individuals prior to entering the covenant of marriage with one another. We were *two broken singles* before we transitioned through marriage into one "*broken couple*." The definition of the word "*couple*" is "*two equal and opposite forces that act along parallel lines.*" Isn't it ironic that the word "**couple**" meaning two, actually refers to two people viewed as "**one unit**?" The bible puts it this way, "**and the two are united as one**" (Genesis 2:24b NLT).

We are on a marriage mission in which we hope to help *couples* and *singles* avoid the pitfalls that nearly hijacked our marriage, bankrupt our relationships with God and one another, derailed our purpose, and destroyed our family. We invite you to join us on this journey leading towards deliverance, healing, strength, and relationship-rebirth. You can prepare by asking yourself the following questions:

- *What is my marital strategy for success (whether currently married or single)?*
- *Am I facing what I would describe as an unimaginable issue in my relationship and do not know where to turn?*
- *Is my marriage on life-support, and I am close to pulling the plug?*
- *Have I become so desperate for change that I'm about ready to accept anything outside of my present situation – whether good or bad?*
- *Why do I feel so bored and resentful in my relationship?*
- *Why do I cheat?*
- *Why do I feel I married the wrong person?*

- How did my parent's (strong, weak, or non-existent) marriage/relationship influence my marital/relationship views and standards?
- Are my premarital, environmental, or cultural differences to blame for my and my spouse's growing resentment and distance toward one another?
- When it comes to my own marriage, am I pleased with the example I'm setting for my family and others?
- Am I about ready to give up and walk away from my marriage and family with the intention of saving what's left of myself?
- Do I feel I have been driven towards emotional "dehydration" due to the countless tears and disappointments I've had to endure in my marriage?
- Do I find myself **fearfully** preparing to marry for the first, second, or more times because I have no idea how to be the "husband" or "wife" I desire to be?

If you can personally identify with one or more of the previous questions, you are not alone! We too struggled with some of these questions many years ago ourselves. Our situation also appeared lifeless…but God! It was not until we made the best decision of our lives that things drastically changed for the best. We gave Jesus all the broken, fragmented pieces of our individual issues along with our collective marital challenges. As a result, we continuously glean from His miraculous transformation and unlimited blessings to this day.

We have no doubt that there are many couples experiencing serious marital trials. Most want to save their marriage, but feel they have exhausted every ounce of their ability to fight for their marriage. Some feel as though their marital problems outweigh their "**marital power**," but that is a lie. You two are more powerful together than as single individuals as stated in the following scriptures, "*I also tell you this: If two of you agree here on earth concerning anything you ask, my Father in heaven will do it for you. For where two or three gather together as my followers, I am there among them*" (Matthew 18:19-20 NLT). If you have questions – God has answers! Therefore, "*Trust in the Lord with all thine heart; and lean not unto thine* *own understanding. In all thy ways acknowledge him, and he shall direct thy paths"* (Proverbs 3:5-6).

By His power, guidance, and wisdom we desire to be the vehicles through which God helps broken individuals transition from victims to victors. Our goal is to strengthen couples, revive marriages, bless families, and glorify God. We are excited as it is our purpose and plan to provide you with a wealth of life transitioning strategies and techniques, to catapult your marriage and family, and live the life you've dreamed of living; and God desires for you to experience. If you are on board with us, repeat this prayer:

"Lord God, I desire the blessed life you purposed for me to live, and want to be in right standing with you. Therefore, I confess and repent of all my unintentional as well as intentional sins, and ask for your forgiveness, cleansing, healing, and restoration. I receive Jesus Christ into my heart. I not only give you myself, but I also surrender my spouse to you as well (by faith if you are not married yet). I submit to your Word as the final authority concerning my relationship with You, and my marital relationship with my spouse.

I thank you in advance for ordering my steps in the direction that is wise, favorable, and progressive for every area of my life, in Jesus' name…amen."

Praise God…now let's grow!

CHAPTER 1

FINDING HIS RIB & RECEIVNG HER RACK

> "Then the Lord God said, 'It is not good for man to be alone. I will make a helper who is just right for him.' v. 21) So the Lord God caused the man to fall into a deep sleep. While the man slept, the Lord God took out one of the man's ribs and closed up the opening. Then the Lord God made a woman from the rib, and he brought her to the man."
>
> *(Genesis 2:18,21 NLT)*

RICHARD FINDS HIS "RIB"

One night while out with a friend, I met a beautiful young lady that caught my attention the moment I laid eyes on her. I introduced myself to her and struck up a conversation. During our chat, I made it a point to be upfront with her. I revealed that I had made some bad choices that resulted in me spending some time in prison. I was relieved at how well she reacted. She was calm and encouraging. She did not hesitate to let me know that she had made some bad choices in her past as well that resulted in painful consequences. Yet, she went on to share how everything changed when she began to trust and follow Jesus Christ, and was now a born-again believer. She was not judgmental and seemed very easy to talk to. She was very confident, but not prideful or arrogant. Even when she divulged that she was a single parent of four daughters she did not speak shamefully; and rightfully so.

Learning that she had children was not a deterrent for me. She was a single parent working and going to school, yet raising four daughters in the Lord. The fact that she seemed to value her family was impressive to me. She presented herself very well. It quickly became obvious to me that she loved and respected God, her children, and herself. Talking with her was very encouraging and somewhat soothing. I admit it was her looks that attracted me to her. But it would ultimately be her encouragement, sense of humor, and commitment to God that would quickly capture my heart, and cause me to fall in love.

For our first date, she invited me to church. This was the first time any woman had ever invited me to church. It was there I saw her brother Aaron. He and I are the same age which is a couple of years older than Renda. As we introduced ourselves to one another, we quickly realized we all had attended the same elementary and middle school together. About eighteen years had passed, so Renda and I initially did not recognize one another. Ironically, I later learned she had once had a huge crush on me when we were kids.

Renda introduced me to her four daughters. When I introduced Renda and her girls to my son Brandon, everyone seemed to get along well. I had never met a woman like Renda before. She never let a conversation end without encouraging me in some way or another. I found myself looking forward to spending time with her and the girls as often as I could. About a month had gone by, when one day I heard God speak to me about Renda and the girls. He said, "*Take care of them and I will bless you.*"

Hearing that from God was a blessing itself. I had already fallen in love with her, and the girls stole my heart the day I met them. By this time, Renda also made it clear that she was in love with me as well. I wasted no time asking Renda to marry me, and she said yes. I had also asked for and received her mother's permission to do so.

To be honest – there were family and friends who were very skeptical about me marrying Renda. They said that I did not know her that well, which was true, but it was mostly because she had children. Some referred to her children as what some call "baggage," but I never once thought of the children as baggage. To me they were little girls with big hearts. These girls, no different than any other children, needed a loving, active, hands-on father, willfully present in their lives on a consistent basis. I never viewed them as burdens – but blessings and eventually "lifesavers" for me! Despite the naysayers and negative feedback from some, Renda and I were married and proceeded on with optimism. I had finally gotten what I had desired and looked forward to for many years – a beautiful family of my own.

Marrying Renda gave me a huge sense of relief. It was the second greatest decision I had ever made, only second to giving my heart to Jesus Christ. Being with her was refreshing to say the least. I no longer had to be concerned with finding a loving wife and having a family. My mission had been accomplished.

Renda not only told me she loved me, but showed it as well. More importantly, she loved the Lord. Her unwavering commitment to the Lord and her purpose was very attractive to me. She was good for me, and to me. I felt blessed to have found her as expressed in Proverbs 18:22, "*Whoso findeth a wife findeth a good thing, and obtaineth favor of the Lord.*" God had fulfilled my dream and His word simultaneously by leading me to Renda – my "rib."

RENDA RECEIVES HER "RACK"

"*Lord, if you don't ever send me a husband, and it's just you and I and the girls – I'm okay with that.*" These were the words I had sincerely spoken to God after He had delivered me from a seven-year relationship that He had warned me to *avoid-like-the-plague* – but I did not listen. So, in all honesty, I did not think I was worthy of God sending me a husband. There I was, a single mother of four who had blatantly ignored God's voice and avoided His guidance for years. So why would I have the nerve to think that God would not push the desires of my heart to the back of the line the way I had done His voice for the previous seven years? I even had folks in the church tell me how slim-to-none my chances were of ever getting married due to my "baggage" as some would say – but God!

After exiting a relationship, starting a new job, and re-entering school, things appeared to finally be falling into place in my life. I was now focused on what was most important. Rebuilding and strengthening my relationship with the Lord, and raising my girls were my top priority. I had envisioned building a legacy for my little ladies, and knew I had a lot of work ahead of me. I did not want, nor did I have time for any distractions. Therefore, I made a commitment to God to stay committed and attentive to fulfilling His purpose for my life, even though I thought that probably meant I would have to do so "solo." But I am so glad that God's ways and thoughts always have been, and always will be higher (Isaiah 55:9).

One evening, my niece who is a hair stylist agreed to "fit-me-in" to do my hair. Once she finished, she asked me if I would pick up a take-out dinner for her and another stylist friend. Despite feeling exhausted from my long work day, and a strong

desire to just get my hair done and go straight home –
I agreed. As I waited in the restaurant's **long, slow**
drive-thru line, I contemplated leaving and simply
telling my niece and her stylist friend they would have
to get dinner for themselves – but I had given them
my word. Despite exhaustion and impatience's strong
attempt to influence me to make up some lie as to
why I could not fulfill my promise, I just couldn't do it.
She had honored her end of the deal, so I was
compelled to honor my end as well.

At just the right moment, I looked up and could
just barely see a small fraction of the dine-in area. I
saw a guy standing inside glaring at me through the
window. I must keep it real. I spotted Richard
checking me out as I was "low key" checking him out.
I thought to myself, *"That guy is sexy!"* Yes, you
heard me right; I said he was sexy (I'm just keeping it
real folks!) It was his clean-cut exterior, gorgeous
eyes, baby-smooth skin, and perfectly sculptured
goatee that instantly captured my attention. However,
it was his humility, boldness, respectfulness, and
honesty that enveloped and kept it!

There are many reasons why I have no doubt
that it is truly the second-best relationship (following

my best relationship with Jesus Christ) I have ever had. When we were dating, whether conversating in person or over-the-phone, he always spoke with enthusiasm – never failing to inspire and encourage me. I also liked that I could be transparent with him without fear of condescending responses or judgmental undertones entering our conversations. Best of all, he made me feel safe and secure in every way.

From our first date (in church) through the moment he proposed to me, I knew there was something special about him. He not only embodied courage and zeal, but also instilled security and the audacity to dream bigger within me and our children. To this day I continuously glean from his relentless optimism. I am so grateful God lead me to marry Richard. For me, our marriage expressed God's redemptive power and solidified his sufficient grace. Also, it simultaneously outmaneuvered satan's strategy to convince me that I was undeserving of a blessed husband and awesome marriage. I had no idea how that one decision to *press my way* to keep my word, as well as being a blessing to others, would change the entire trajectory of my life. In the process of doing so, I was led to my husband or as I always say, my "rack" – Richard.

School-of-Love-and-Marriage

This chapter, "*Finding His Rib & Receiving Her Rack*" painted a joyful, exciting, flattering, and inspiring portrait of our union. Although encouraging, the previous section is merely a prelude of our love and marriage. At a glance, it may appear to imply that no effort or "work" was required from neither of us; but nothing could be further from the truth. Little did we know – that would only be a "snapshot" of the beginning!

Exchanging vows (legally) made it official. We had become partners, as well as students, in the **School-of-Love-and-Marriage**. We "registered" by falling in love, and "paid tuition" by saying, "I do." It launched the beginning of our partnership in the lifelong course we like to call "Love Lessons." No different from any other course, we must consistently study, and *actually "do the work"* to ensure our success.

29

We consider this book a "study guide" to relationship development and marital success. Someone reading this may be thinking, *"Does it really take all of that? Is it even worth it?"* Only you can determine that answer as it pertains to you and your relationship. However, we can attest that although our labor-of-love was at times inconvenient and undeniably painful, it undoubtedly was necessary and worth it! To this day, it continues to grant us access to the limitless harvests God's Word promises,

*"So let's not get tired of doing what is good. At just the right time we will reap a harvest of blessing if we **don't give up**"* (Galatians 6:9 NLT.)

If you and your spouse feel you have failed too many tests in the "Love Lessons" course – don't give up hope! What we sometimes view as "tests," are only quizzes. So be encouraged. Do not make the mistake of putting a "period" in the place where God put a "comma." As you will see ahead, what we often view as a bad ending, can be a camouflage for a blessed, new beginning.

CHAPTER 2

LIVING & LOVING STRATEGICALLY

> "For I know the plans I have for you,"
> says the Lord. "They are plans for
> good and not for disaster, to give you
> a future and a hope."
>
> (Jeremiah 29:11 NLT)

A Strategist is defined as a person who is skilled in making plans for achieving a goal: someone who is good at forming strategies. God is the Master Strategist and the Architect for *Strategic Living*. He planned and created the heavens and the earth (Genesis 1:1, John 1:1-3). He also planned and created mankind in His own image (Genesis 1:26-27). God designed and instructed us to live life His way as a wise and powerful strategist, to successfully produce and prosper in the earth stress-free (Genesis 1:28-30).

God, the Master Strategist and Architect, also set the standard for decency and order (1st Corinthians 14:40). So much so, that he constructed and produced precise "*blueprints*" for living and loving strategically. They are purposed to ensure man's successful, stress-free navigation through life and love. One's ability to stay-the-course relies on his or her understanding of the God-given strategist mandate, and one's willingness to obey (Jeremiah 23:11, Proverbs 16:1, 16:3, 16:9).

THE MASTER'S BLUEPRINT FOR MAN'S LIFE

A *blueprint* is a detailed, visual plan of how to do something. We get our first glimpse of the Master Architect's *"Strategic-Living Blueprint"* for man's life in the first chapter of Genesis. As you read the blueprint, take notice that its structure consists of two components – *planning* and *implementation*. Also take notice how God Himself first adhered to its components before passing them along to man:

PLANNING

> *"And God said, Let us make man in our image, after our likeness: and let them have dominion over the fish of the sea, and over the fowl of*

the air, and over the cattle, and over all the
earth, and over every creeping thing that
creepeth upon the earth. (Genesis 1:26)

IMPLEMENTATION

> ➤ *(27) So God created man in his own image, in*
> *the image of God created he him; male and*
> *female created he them. (28) And God blessed*
> *them, and God said unto them, Be fruitful and*
> *multiply, and replenish the earth, and subdue*
> *it: and have dominion over the fish of the sea,*
> *and over the fowl of the air, and over every*
> *living thing that moveth upon the earth."*
> (Genesis 1:27-28)

Furthermore, the bible states in Proverbs 4:7,
"Wisdom is the principle thing; therefore get wisdom:
and with all thy getting get understanding." That
being said, grasping the wisdom of the two
components of *planning* and *implementation* is
important; and so is getting an understanding of what
it is one plans to implement. In short, what good is a
blueprint if you lack the understanding of it?
Therefore, let us begin by taking a closer look at

some "key" words within the Strategic-Living Blueprint, in order to unlock a clearer perspective:

1. Image – representation of the function or external form of a person
2. Likeness – to resemble quality
3. Dominion – absolute ownership
4. Create – to bring something into existence
5. Blessed – empower to prosper
6. Fruitful – to be fertile
7. Multiply – to greatly increase in number
8. Replenish – to fill with inspiration and power
9. Subdue – to bring under subjection or submission

Now let us replace the "key" words within the blueprint with their definitions, and reread them in layman terms. This put God's Strategic-Living Blueprint in a clearer, and even more retainable perspective for us, and we believe it will do the same for you:

"**God _brought man into existence_ to be a _representation of His function in external form_, to resemble his presence and bring forth the qualities of his being. He gave man _absolute_** *ownership* **of the whole earth to** *influence and reign over it,* **and every animal in it. God** *brought male and female into existence,* **to** *establish a representation of His function in external form* **in the earth. He** *empowered them to prosper,* **instructed them to be** *fertile (physically and spiritually), and to* *greatly increase in number by reproducing.* **God further instructed man to** *fill the earth with his inspiration and power,* **and** *keep it under subjection.* **He gave man** *absolute ownership* **over all the animals in the earth."** (Genesis 1:26-28)

This not only provides wisdom and understanding of the Strategic-Living Blueprint, but also an answer to the question many have asked for centuries, *"What is man's purpose?"*

God is sovereign as well as strategic. The bible states that God made humans (male and female) in His own *image*. The word "image" in this particular text is often referred to God's appearance, when in addition, it is in reference to His way of "functioning" as translated (tselem) in Hebrew. The word function has a two-fold definition:

1. Function – a precise purpose or action for which a person or thing exists.
2. Function – to operate

God is strategic and so is His love. Therefore, we, humans made in His image, are to reflect God's way of functioning in life, love, and Marriage.

THE MASTER'S BLUEPRINT FOR MARRIAGE

Just as God crafted a blueprint for life, such was the same for Marriage. The Garden of Eden, chosen as the "birthplace of life," was also the designated venue for the **birth of marriage**. As God, the Master Strategist and Architect, presented the *Master's Blueprint for Marriage*, He remained consistent in upholding the two components – *planning and implementation*:

PLANNING

> *"Then the Lord God said, "It is not good for the man to be alone. I will make a **helper** who is **just right for him**." (Genesis 2:18 NLT)*

IMPLEMENTATION

➤ *"So the Lord God caused the man to fall into a deep sleep. While the man slept, the Lord God took out one of the man's ribs and closed up the opening. Then the Lord God **made a woman from the rib**, and **he brought her to the man**. 'At last!' the man exclaimed. 'This **one** is bone of my bone, and flesh of my flesh! She will be called 'woman,' because she was taken from 'man.' This explains why a man leaves his father and mother and is joined to his wife, and **the two are united as one**."* (Genesis 2:21-24 NLT)

God created marriage. His word substantiates its foundation, purpose, and intent. Contrary to many misguided theories, God's Word cannot be altered, manipulated, or redefined by man's personal opinions or choices. Despite man's insistence for expressing his or her wavering opinions and undisciplined choices, these opinions and choices are subject to error. Therefore, it is imperative that we understand the biblical birth of marriage, and how its' original

GOD'S PURPOSE FOR MARRIAGE

It is here in Genesis 2:18 where God began by referring to "man" in the singular form meaning "one." It is also here where God clearly states His purpose for marriage – **God did not want man** (Adam) **to be alone.** You may ask, "*In what way did God mean 'alone'?*" We are glad you asked that question! Genesis 1:26-29 supplies the answers. It is here that God referred to "man" in the plural form meaning "*two or more.*" So, God did not want man (Adam) to be alone in the following ten areas:

> ➢ Representation – reflecting God's way of functioning, and resembling his presence in the earth.
> ➢ Domination – executing absolute ownership and authority over all the animals in the earth, in which each animal itself was created with a counterpart.

- ➢ Creation – bringing things such as human beings, ideas, and inventions into existence, as God (the Father, the Son, and Holy Spirit) does.
- ➢ Empowerment – the authority and capability to be successful.
- ➢ Reproduction – Childbirth
- ➢ Multiplication – increase greatly (male and female).
- ➢ Provision – fill the earth with man's influence and power, and supply the governors to do so.
- ➢ Cultivation – to bring under subjection.
- ➢ Maintenance – continuously maintain or hold on to your absolute ownership and authority over all the animals.
- ➢ Nutrition – to be a catalyst for great physical and spiritual health and wellness.

In conclusion, God's marital standard should be the unshakable foundation of every marriage. As "junior" strategists created in God's image and likeness, God intends for man (male and female) to use the powerful Strategic Living and Loving Blueprints He supplied. Husband and wife are purposed to master, thrive, influence, and "grow" forward in all ten areas together in marriage – as <u>one</u> unit or team.

CHAPTER 3

RESTORING THE LENSES-OF-LOVE

> *"At last!" the man exclaimed. This one is bone from my bone, and flesh from my flesh! She will be called 'woman,' because she was taken from 'man.' This explains why a man leaves his father and mother and is joined to his wife, and the two are united into one."*
>
> *(Genesis 2:23 NLT)*

God's view and intent for marriage remains the same for man today, as it did for Adam and Eve in the beginning. It was not only instituted to unite man and woman physically in unison with one another, but also spiritually in unison with God. It is a pleasurable strength – not a hindering weakness. **It was to enhance their ability to envision, understand, and fulfill their God-given purpose in the earth**. Therefore, it only makes sense that satan would formulate the *strategy of visual detachment* to secure the opposite effect.

Visual Detachment:

a. The act or *process* of visually separating something from a larger thing; resulting in an overall decrease. (Spiritually)

b. A lack of emotion or of personal interest. (Physically)

Case-in-point #1:

In Genesis 3, the woman allows herself to be influenced by satan, by way of the serpent (that she had ownership and authority over by the way), to disobey God by eating from the forbidden tree. She then influenced the man and he disobeyed God and ate from the forbidden tree as well. When they were confronted by God, both replied with sinful compulsion. First, Adam was asked if he had eaten from the forbidden tree. Adam replied,

*"It was **the woman you gave me** who gave me the fruit, and I ate it"* (Genesis 3:12 NLT).

Notice Adam immediately responded with **visual detachment**. In that moment, he saw her as one who was "**given to him**", and no longer the (unique) one who was "**created out of him.**" His initial reaction was a futile attempt to detach himself from the woman, or as he called her, "*bone of my bone, and flesh of my flesh,*" as well as from the repercussions of his own personal choice. He had the opportunity to respond with a simple "yes," and could have taken responsibility for his own decision to disobey God. Instead, he attempted to totally '*individualize*' and **protect** himself by playing the "blame-game."

You may be thinking, "*How could he just detach himself from her so coldly and quickly without even thinking about it?*" This was because he had willfully partaken in sin. And as stated in James 1:15, sin produces death, although not necessarily immediate *physical* death, spiritual death is certain. It is a deadening of the spiritual senses or **enhanced ability to envision, understand, and fulfill your God-given purpose in the earth**.

Sin is a liar and a thief, and Adam had fallen victim to its grip. This is why he could no longer see her the same as before. Prior to engaging in sin, Adam viewed her through the clear spiritual lenses of pure love – God's *"authentic"* love. No obstructions or distractions of the flesh were present.

Up to this point, Adam had continually walked in the spirit, and did not have to battle his flesh. So, when he first laid eyes on Eve, he fell in love with her spirit and became one with her flesh. After their fall, they no longer walked with the spirit of God, so it was literally effortless for him to fulfil the lusts of the flesh (Galatians 5:16). Therefore, his "lenses-of-love" were replaced with views of lusts as stated in 1 John 2:16, *"For all that is in the world, the lust of the flesh and the lust of the eyes, and the pride of life, is not of the Father, but is of the world."*

1 Corinthians 13:4-7 explains what "authentic" love is. For example, love is not self-seeking or selfish. However, sin is everything love is not. Sin's very foundation is "self-seeking." If sin had a motto, it would sound something like: *"It's all about me!"*

Not only did Adam try to detach from Eve, but disown her as well. He candidly referred to her as, **"The woman you gave me,"** as if she was never a part of him, and the two were never joined as one.

He no longer referred to *her* as "*bone of my bone, and flesh of my flesh.*" His wife literally went from "**a helper that is just right**" for him, to "**the woman you gave me**" in an instant!

Disappointment did not appear to be present when Adam learned Eve disobeyed God by eating from the forbidden tree to begin with, nor when she presented the opportunity for him to join her in the act of disobedience. However, it is at the moment of his confrontation with God that Adam appears disappointed and unappreciative of Eve and God for the first time. Adam literally blamed both Eve and God for his bad decision to sew 'sin' into the fabric of his life. Isn't it ironic that he did not at all appear to be disappointed with himself?

You may be asking, "*Where did Adam get that foolishness from?*" His behavior was a direct extension of the root of sin. Needless to say, the "blame-game" is one of its fruit. As a result, the lenses-of-sin only reflect the faults of others – not one's self.

Case-in-point #2

Eve's confrontation with God was no better. When God asked her what had she done, she followed Adam's lead and equally replied by way of the "blame game." She blamed the serpent for influencing her to eat from the forbidden tree, and took no personal responsibility for her own decision to doubt, dishonor, and disobey God. She was completely out of order – literally. So much so, her actions disrupted God's perfect order of "dominion" he had given man.

Initially, man (Adam and Eve) had dominion over all the animals, the earth, and more importantly – their own flesh. Outside of God, they were not subject to any of the animals or anything in the earth. In fact, they were anointed to *influence* and *control* the animals, not the other way around. But instead, Eve allowed satan, by way of a serpent, to influence her to doubt God and sin. She then transferred her influence and authority over to the very thing she was purposed to rule over. In doing so, she was the first to willingly replace her "lenses-of-love" for lenses-of-sin. Furthermore, she had allowed herself to become *bait* for Adam to follow suit and relinquish his influence and authority as well.

You may be thinking, "*How could she even consider doing something like that?*" It was because of doubt. Doubt is the prelude to disobedience. Show us a person who doubts God's word, and we'll show a person who will dishonor it. Once Eve decided to doubt God, her dishonorable behavior toward God and Adam was inevitable. This is because one cannot honor whom one has lost respect for.

Eve, not Adam, was the first to become "deadened" to her **enhanced ability to envision, understand, and fulfill their God-given purpose in the earth**. When she had sewn 'sin' into the fabric of her life, she surrendered her "*influential anointing*" from God, for two of the deadliest fruit that extends from the root of sin – manipulation and deceit. These came forth by way of dishonor. She no longer saw her husband as her honorable and respected "rack," nor as the (unique) one in which she was created from and purposed to "co-rule" with. She was no longer focused on "helping" him. Instead, her primary interest had shifted from equaling ruling with him, to possibly ruling *over* him through manipulation and deceit.

This was one of the very reasons that God instructed man (Adam and Eve) not to eat from the tree of the Knowledge of Good and Evil. He knew that once they were exposed to "self-seeking" sin, the spouse they use to view as an asset, they would now view as a liability!

God's ***original intent*** for marriage has not changed, but unfortunately the mindset of many people has. The perspective of marriage as a liability instead of an asset, appears to be the sentiment of many males and females today. Many in our current society have accepted a manipulated, distorted, and diluted view of marriage; in an effort to render its guidelines negotiable. As a result, what God has rejected as an abomination, some have accepted as a blessing. The bible warns of this dangerous path,

"There is a path before each person that seems right, but it ends in death." (Proverbs 14:12, 16:25 NLT)

It is vital that we view marriage through God's "microscope of marriage" (His Word), despite the feelings and opinions of many that suggest the contrary. Because it all boils down to this fact, *"We may throw the dice, but the Lord determines how they fall.*" (Proverbs 16:33 NLT)

THE CURSE IS REVERSED

When all was said and done, all parties involved in the fall of man, including the serpent, reaped a curse that would envelope them and their offspring for generations to come (Genesis 3:14-19). The entire ordeal set the stage for what we believe was the original "hard-knock-life." There would be no getting around it. This meant all born into the earth following man's fall, would literally have to battle their flesh from the moment he or she enters the world.

You or someone you know may have uttered, "*If that were me in that garden, things would have gone differently.*" Or maybe you thought, "*Why should I have to suffer when I wasn't even there? I wish there was something that could be done to undo the damage.*" Thing is, you don't have to suffer any longer, because the damage has already been repaired!

GOD'S PERFECT MARITAL STRATEGY

Marriage is both spiritual and physical. God, being the Master Strategist that He is, established the perfect strategy to reverse-the-curse and restore the lenses-of-love in how we view life and love spiritually, in order to properly execute it physically. He did so by continuing with the two components of *planning* and *implementation*:

PLANNING

> ➢ *The Lord God said to the serpent*, "*Because you have done this, you are cursed more than all the cattle, and more than any animal of the field; on your belly you shall go, and dust you shall eat all the days of your life. And I will put enmity (open hostility) between you and the woman, and between your seed (offspring)* **and her Seed; He shall [fatally] bruise your head, and you shall [only] bruise His heel.**" (Genesis 3:14-15 AMP)

IMPLEMENTATION

> *"This is how much God loved the world:* **He gave** *his* **Son, his one and only Son.** *And this is why: so that no one need be destroyed; by believing in him, anyone can have a* <u>whole</u> *and lasting life. God didn't go to all the trouble of sending his Son merely to point an accusing finger, telling the world how bad it was.* **He came to help, to put the world right again.** *Anyone who trusts in him is acquitted; anyone who refuses to trust him has long since been under the death sentence without knowing it."* (John 3:16-18 MSG)

The 'lenses' in which one uses to view marriage, especially one's own, should not be determined by one's personal interpretation of *"What would Jesus do if He were married to my spouse?"* It should be based on the example Jesus set in the way in which He treats His bride (the church), as well as the spiritual and physical boundaries and standards set by the Word of God regarding the marriage of man (man and woman):

"Wives, be subject to your own husbands, as [a service] to the Lord. For the husband is head of the wife, as Christ is head of the church, Himself being the Savior of the body. But as the church is subject to Christ, so also wives should be subject to their husbands in everything [respecting both their position as protector and their responsibility to God as head of the house]. Husbands, love your wives [seek the highest good for her and surround her with a caring, unselfish love], just as Christ also loved the church and gave Himself up for her, so that He might sanctify the church, having cleansed her by the washing of water with the word [of God], so that [in turn] He might present the church to himself in glorious splendor, without spot or wrinkle or any such thing; but that she would be holy [set apart for God] and blameless. Even so husbands should and are morally obligated to love their own wives as [being in a sense] their own bodies. He who loves his own wife loves himself. For no one ever hated his own body, but [instead] he nourishes and protects and cherishes it, just as Christ does the church, because we are members (parts) of

His body. FOR THIS REASON A MAN SHALL LEAVE HIS FATHER AND HIS MOTHER AND SHALL BE JOINED [and be faithfully devoted] TO HIS WIFE, AND THE TWO SHALL BECOME ONE FLESH. This mystery [of two becoming one] is great; but I am speaking with reference to [the relationship of] Christ and the church. However, each man among you [without exception] is to love his wife as his very own self [with behavior worthy of respect and esteem, always seeking the best for her with an attitude of lovingkindness], and the wife [must see to it] that she respects and delights in her husband [that she notices him and prefers him and treats him with loving concern, treasuring him, honoring him, and holding him dear] (Ephesians 5:22-32 AMP).

CHAPTER 4

DON'T DIVORCE OVER CORNED BEEF & CABBAGE

> *But it was to us that God revealed these things by His Spirit. For His Spirit searches out everything and shows us God's deep secrets.*
>
> *(1st Corinthians 2:10 NLT)*

Once we began dating, things moved quickly. We literally married within six to eight weeks later (we strongly do not recommend this to others.) We had not been married long when we almost allowed "corned beef and cabbage" to escort us into divorce court. Seriously! We literally almost divorced over a disagreement over corned beef and cabbage! We know it is hard to believe, but it's true. Let us explain.

Marrying so quickly, there were still quite a few things we did not know about one another, and some things we hadn't yet learned about ourselves. Our family backgrounds and life-experiences were quite different, still we failed to get counseling prior to marriage. Although we believed we were being led by

God, our failure to seek godly counsel put us at a disadvantage. We thank God that we had people of God praying for us during that time, because we weren't exactly sure what to do, or what we were doing.

One day, Richard asked me if I would cook corned beef and cabbage for dinner the following evening – I agreed. However, while growing up, my only experience with corned beef as a meal, was on onion roll or rye bread within a sandwich. Yet, Richard's experience with corned beef as a meal, was to mix it with cabbage. So, imagine my surprise when I received the request from him. I thought to myself, *"He wants a corned beef sandwich with cabbage on-the-side...that's weird, but fine – I'll make it for him."*

The following morning, we had some sort of minor disagreement. But back then, I could hold an attitude like it had handles! So, I didn't really talk to him much throughout that day. After preparing the corned beef, I had everything set up just right – so I thought. I had the corned beef, onion rolls, rye bread, mustard, and cabbage-on-the-side.

As I stood in the kitchen getting ready to gather his food onto a plate, I thought, *"Who in their right mind would want to eat a corned beef* **sandwich** *with cabbage-on-the-side?"* I then made eye contact with him as he glared at me from the bottom of the basement stairs. *"Which bread do you want for your sandwich,"* I asked. *"What did you just ask me?"* He sarcastically responded. Being an inexperienced newlywed wife (yet independent thinker), from a long line of strong-willed women; I did not appreciate the tone in which he responded, so I sarcastically repeated, *"Which bread do you want for your corned beef* **sandwich***?"* He replied, *"So you're trying to be funny huh?"*

At that point, I was totally confused and not sure what I had done to upset him. Adding insult to injury, he then came upstairs into the kitchen and proceeded to complain about how I had failed to properly prepare the corned beef and cabbage. He went on to say, *"What woman with common sense doesn't know how to cook corned beef and cabbage the right way?"* I responded, *"Your mama evidently!"* From that point forward, it was an all-out brutal war of words!

The wise thing to do would have been to calm down, and attempt to defuse the situation. Instead, we started yelling back and forth at each other, which escalated to name calling, insults, and criticizing one another's mother. That led to us both expressing that our marriage may have been a mistake. This resulted in us considering divorce.

We had transformed our mouths into machine guns, and our choice of words supplied the ammunition. Richard felt disrespected, and I felt unappreciated. The entire ordeal could have been prevented from going as far as it did, had we both adhered to Proverbs 15:1 AMP which says, "*A soft and gentle and thoughtful answer turns away wrath, but harsh and painful and careless words stir up anger.*" Had we not both humbled ourselves, and come to our senses, we would have allowed the "little foxes" of anger, pride, unforgiveness, misunderstanding, and resentment to "ruin the vineyards of our love" (Song of Solomon 2:15 NLT).

This is a good example of how a simple misunderstanding can quickly open the door for **visual detachment**. You two, can go from "we" to "me" in an instant, if you don't build on the strong foundation of unity and the Word of God. Both prepare you to act and respond wisely when issues arise – whether big or small. Throughout the years, we have learned that building a great marriage is possible, but it does not stem from a married couple who manages to avoid the little foxes; but from a unified, strategic couple who endures them together and prevails!

THE MICROSCOPE OF MARRIAGE

You or your spouse may have "issues" related to turbulent cultural, personal, marital, sexual, or religious experiences, that have caused you to view marriage in a negative, complicated, confused, or distorted way. These experiences are often the catalyst to one's emotional brokenness and lack of trust towards others, as a "single" – prior to marriage. Ironically, these experiences do not necessarily discourage one from marriage, but can set the stage for an obstructive and divisive view; and weaken the foundation of his or her marital intent.

We experienced some visual obstructions when it came to our own marriage at one time, so we understand its destructive potential. We were fortunate to overcome them through prayer and submission to God (James 4:7), and one another (Ephesians 5:21). We believe the revelation that God used to transform our marriage can do the same for yours, and countless others. We call it '**The Microscope of Marriage**.' It provides an enhanced perspective of how one's culture, life-experiences, principles, and standards (or lack of) can directly influence one's marital views and behaviors for "*better or worse*."

It begins with self-observation. Examining one's self-perception can simultaneously reveal his or her perspective of a spouse as well. For instance, one spouse may see himself or herself as a "single" within the marriage, instead of two joined as <u>one</u> unit. As a result, the opportunity for unity and a "*healthy love*" growth within the marriage, as well as within their future '*bloodline*' is slim-to-none. In order to correct one's (generational) contaminated marital perception, *he or she must locate, examine, and prune his or her own polluted roots*.

LET THE 'GAMES' BEGIN

We will begin by posing some questions. Many tend to jump at the chance to answer question number one, and maybe even question number two. But questions three thru seven often prove to be a bit more challenging. We encourage you to be as open and truthful with yourself, and each other, as possible.

1. Do you and your spouse practice the same faith or religious beliefs? If not, why? Do your beliefs affect your relationship? Do you and your spouse pray together? If so, how often? If not, why?

2. How has your family culture, marital mentors, and past personal experiences influenced your marital beliefs?

3. How has your beliefs contributed to the success or failure of your marriage(s), engagement (s), or past relationship (s)?

4. What do you believe is the purpose for **your** marriage? Does your spouse agree? If not, why?

---

5. Have you and your spouse discussed or formulated a vision or plan for your marriage? If so, what is it? If not, why?
6. Do you and your spouse have the same views about sex? If not, why?
7. Are you content with your family size? If not, why? Is your spouse content? If not, why?

The previous questions can be a starting point for couples to respectfully acknowledge and discuss personal differences plaguing their marriage. It is purposed to promote equal submission, and help both gain a better understanding of one another. In return, it sets the stage for a unified front, to strategically formulate a plan that will result in victory over all the "little foxes."

There are some couples that choose to marry one another, despite their flagrant personal differences. Do to their inability to relate to one another's upbringing, background, traditions, habits, or experiences; they often appear apathetic towards issues that his or her spouse may feel are important. We believe marriage counseling can be beneficial in dealing with many of these issues. Unfortunately, many couples often dismiss the idea of obtaining marriage counseling based on biblical principles, because they believe their strong "love" for each other will somehow make-up for their lack of knowledge. They are often under the misconception that whether they unify within the marriage or not, eventually things will haphazardly fall right into place – which is not typically how things turn out.

When a spouse or spouses become disappointed in the lack of their marital progress, some begin to focus on themselves – aside from his or her spouse, and embrace his or her own *individuality* as a recourse. Their desire for his or her own personal growth and development, as well as pleasurable fulfillment, becomes top priority. Any suggestion of marital unity is now viewed as a setback instead of an advancement. This ideology further encourages a distorted view of marriage. It attempts to redefine marital success as the ability to maintain one's own "individual" identity by way of that "old fox" – ***visual detachment***.

Due to a lack of God's wisdom, the couple then views marital *unity* as a threat to his or her own "personal" power. As a result, a spouse can be mistaken as an enemy, instead of a trusted ally. This demonic strategy deceives a spouse or spouses into constantly operating in a "personal" protection mode. This renders the couple unable to successfully unify, or maximize their supernatural, pinnacle power to be the victorious team God intended for them and their bloodline to be.

Show us a person who has major trust issues with people, and we will show you a person who has trust issues with God. Many are taking their debilitating past hurts, pains, disappointments, and traumas, into their marriages without disclosing the depth and severity. Many of these unsuspecting newlyweds, as well as marital veterans, have been set up for failure without prior knowledge. The only affective remedy for this emotionally terminal condition is Jesus Christ! I cannot stress the following wisdom enough, *"Trust God from the bottom of your heart; don't try to figure out everything on your own. Listen for God's voice in everything you do, and everywhere you go; he's the one who will keep you on track"* (Proverbs 3:5-7 MSG).

THE WILL TO CHANGE

There are many (Christians and non-Christians alike) who are under the misconception that a person who is not willing to change prior to marriage will somehow, miraculously change AFTER marriage. Believing that every bad habit, and non-existent good habit, would somehow switch positions for the welfare of their "legal" unity is willful blindness.

Case-in-point #3:

If one's fiancé has repeatedly been unfaithful to him or her leading up to the marriage ceremony, it's highly unlikely that he or she will stop, and go 'cold turkey' immediately after spewing the words "I do." In a case such as this, one would need the following *spiritual heart* transplant **before** marriage:

PLANNING

> ➤ *"Create in me a **clean heart**, O God. Renew a **loyal** spirit in me."* (Psalms 51:10 NLT)
> ➤ *"But if we confess our sins to Him, he is faithful and just to forgive us our sins and to cleanse us from all wickedness."* (1st John 1:9 NLT)

> ➤ *"Don't copy the behavior and customs of this world,* **but let God transform you into a new person by changing the way you think.** *Then you will learn to know God's will for you, which is good and pleasing and perfect.* (Romans 12:2 NLT)

IMPLEMENTATION

> ➤ *"<u>Don't lie</u> to each other, for you have stripped off your old sinful nature and all its wicked deeds.* **Put on your new nature, and be renewed** *as you* **learn to know your Creator and become more like Him.** *"* (Colossians 3:9-10 NLT)

Furthermore, in conjunction with the much-needed sincere confession of the Word of God in faith, A-C-T-I-O-N is needed to uphold the commitment.

Any marital vows verbalized before a minister, host of family, friends, and more importantly God, is not worth the sheet of paper it's written on without the necessary corresponding actions needed to support it. It's amazing how some people seem to believe that wedding vows are "magical," and provides some sort of "guarantee" that despite no action is taken to change bad behavior, change (for the better) is inevitable. Unfortunately, that is usually not the case at all. Understand this...words can encourage one's behavior, but it takes *action* to change it! In short, James 2:26 says, *"Faith without works is dead."* The same goes for vows without action.

If you happen to fall into the category of those who have never even considered any of the previous questions, don't feel bad. You are not the first, and unfortunately, you will not be the last. It is not surprising when you look at the current rise in the number of couples who think marriage counseling is "old fashioned," and do not feel it is necessary. In fact, many people in this present day could probably attest that they receive most of their relationship advice from family, friends, reality TV shows, social media, or movies with unhealthy views and experiences regarding marriage. Therefore, a number of marital relationships are bound to suffer greatly, due to the rejection of God's wisdom and knowledge.

As a result, countless families are at risk of being negatively impacted for generations to come, if correction and change isn't implemented. However, there is hope for those who choose to seek and trust in God's wisdom as Proverbs 3:5-7 NLT instructs,

"Trust in the Lord with all your heart; do not depend on your own understanding. Seek his will in all you do, and he will show you which path to take."

Don't pretend to know it all, or act as though you've had the answers all along. Don't continue to wander aimlessly and expect things to fall into place by happenstance. Take this opportunity to surrender yourselves and your marriage to God. Allow yourselves to learn and understand better – in order to do better and live happy. Humble yourselves and go to God together in prayer as stated in 1 Peter 5:7 AMP,

"Therefore humble yourselves under the mighty hand of God [set aside self-righteous pride], so that He may exalt you [to a place of honor in His service] at the appropriate time, casting all your cares [all your anxieties, all your worries, and all your concerns, once and for all] on Him, for He cares about you [with deepest affection, and watches over you very carefully] (1 Peter 5:7 AMP).

Furthermore, stop listening to foolishness. Shut down all portals that deliver that destructive rhetoric, and position yourselves to reap the blessings of God (Proverbs 1:1-3). For those currently facing marital challenges due to a lack of counseling, or severe and overwhelming marital issues, we strongly encourage you two, to seek Holy Bible-based marital counseling for assistance.

CHAPTER 5

THE POWER OF AN INFLUENTIAL MAN

> "Husbands, love your wives [seek the highest good for her and **surround her with a caring, unselfish love**], just as Christ also loved the church and gave Himself up for her.
>
> (Ephesians 5:25 AMP)

F ear began to envelope me as I laid there motionless, and unable to move. Feeling groggy, anxious, and in quite a bit of pain after having surgery, all I could I do was moan. I could barely see, and was unable to visually focus. As I began breathing faster and deeper I heard, "*Relax baby, I'm right here,*" coming from my husband. I did not have to physically lay eyes on him. Just hearing Richard's voice, immediately soothed me. No more anxiety or fear. In an instant, peace had been restored to my spirit, mind, and body as described in Psalms 3:5 NLT, "*I lay down and slept, yet I woke up in safety, for the Lord was watching over me."* (Psalms 3:5 NLT). This was so because I knew without a shadow of doubt - I was safe!

God is the Master Creator. His creations are limitless. Yet one of the most fascinating of all, is His creation known as "**safety**." The word *safety* means *"to protect or secure against failure, breakage, or accident."* The interesting thing about this word 'safety,' is that it doubles as a noun (person, place, or thing) and a verb (shows action). It also varies in its method of operation, such as its form, shape, and size, but its universal purpose remains unchanged – to **ensure protection or security**.

The bible clearly shows us that Christ is the "Safety" for His bride (the church). Likewise, husbands are the "safety" for their wives:

*"Husbands, love your wives [seek the highest good for her and **<u>surround</u> her with a caring, unselfish love**], just as Christ also loved the church and gave Himself up for her. (Ephesians 5:25 AMP)*

For a woman, the most valuable and influential asset a man possesses, is his ability to make her feel *"protected and secured against failure, breakage, or an accident."* Whether physically, emotionally, or financially or otherwise – security is a woman's top priority within a relationship. It is not by coincidence that it is the first instruction given to husbands, in that chapter. Richard, has served as my 'safety' for many years now. I praise God for my husband's unselfish, sincere commitment and diligence *"to protect and secure (me) against failure, breakage, or accident,"* in various ways.

SAFETY BLANKET
= a husband who covers and comforts his wife when she is weak or vulnerable.

As I was being taken to my semi-private room, Richard expressed that he loved me, and how he came prepared to stay overnight and personally take care of me. One of the nurses responded with blatant disdain, *"That won't be necessary! Your wife will only be here one night, so there is no need to overreact! Besides, hospital policy does not allow it for patients in semi-private rooms."* That only seemed to encourage Richard more. He prayed, and then decided to go the extra mile and take his request to management. He explained how he was aware of the hospital's policy against overnight visitor's in semi-private rooms. He went on to say that he did not mind sleeping in a chair in one of the waiting rooms if possible, as long as he could be there for me whenever I needed him.

God gave him favor with the managers. So much so, they transferred me to a private room at no extra cost, and Richard stayed in the room with me overnight. I knew he was exhausted, so I assured him that I would be fine, and encouraged him to go home and get some rest. *"Nope,"* he insisted! He went on to say, *"I'm not leaving you here all night by yourself. I'm staying here to help and make sure you will be alright. The nurses have other patients, and may not be able to get to you fast as you may need them to. I love you honey, so I'm not going anywhere."*

He greeted the nurses (on all shifts), and let them know that he would be staying overnight. He told them he was there to assist me with as much as he could, without getting in their way. The nurses and I both were glad to have him there to help. He helped with everything from feeding and bathing me, to bathroom transfers and combing my hair. He also prayed for, and with me. Despite the physical pain I was in, I managed to rest well as stated in Psalms 16:9 NLT, *"No wonder my heart is glad, and I rejoice. My body rests in safety."* Many of the hospital staff and visitors complimented him for willfully taking such good care of me.

He continued to care of me no differently at home. Despite my angry outbursts due to the pain I was experiencing during weeks of recovery, he pretty much took care of everyone and everything. Furthermore, he continuously did so without murmuring or complaining. He cared for our kids, worked, cooked, cleaned, and served at church as well. Our family, friends, and many others were inspired by his passion, and level of intentional commitment to take care of me, and our family. I was extremely thankful to God and Richard, for providing my heart's desire – securely covering me on every level.

SAFETY NET

= a husband who provides security against difficulty or failure.

After my recovery process, I began to ponder over it all. My love and appreciation for all my husband had done, and continued to do; was overwhelming. I asked, "*Lord, why me? What made you want to bless me with a husband like Richard? I don't cook consistently for him, and when he asks me to cook more – I make excuses or complain. I don't show him as much appreciation as I should. Why would he want to cater to me the way that he does, without complaining, when I don't do half the things I could do to make things easier for him?*"

God replied, "*Richard humbled himself, and received my unconditional love; and is appreciative of it. He willingly submitted and committed himself to me. Jesus lives in and through his heart. Therefore, he desires to take the best care of you because he loves and desires you; just as Jesus takes the best care of (His bride) the church, because He loves and desires her. He sacrifices for you, because Jesus sacrificed for the church. He had no problem washing and cleaning you up physically, just as Jesus washed and cleansed the church spiritually. Richard takes care of you as if he were taking care of himself,* *because just as Christ and the church are one – you two also are <u>one</u>.*

God has since given me an even greater revelation. God is love (1st John 4:8), and love covers numerous faults (1st Peter 4:8). A husband walking in his influential anointing is purposed to reflect the love of God, by "blanketing" his wife with unconditional love when she errors. When the church errors, Christ's does not detach from her, yet covers her with grace. He does not humiliate or embarrass her. An influential husband covers his wife in public, corrects her in private, assists her with love and patience, as he strengthens her in prayer. He understands that an atmosphere of security, creates a climate for her successful recovery.

SAFETY HARNESS

= a husband who embraces his wife with the Fruit of the Spirit to protect her from falling or injury.

I wish I could say that my lack of cooking was my only downfall, but there have been others. There were times when I "missed-the-mark" spiritually, financially, and emotionally as well. I have had to humble myself more times than I would like to mention, yet God and Richard both showed me compassion and love.

There was a time when I had deep roots of unforgiveness and contention in my heart, yet Richard refused to "feed the monsters" so-to-speak. He would pray for me, and even with me, but he would not entertain my foolishness. And foolishness it was. Proverbs 14:1 warns, *"A wise woman builds her house, but a foolish woman tears it down with her own hands,"* or in my case – my own mouth! I could not see, or even hear myself behaving as badly as I was. But no matter how contentiously I behaved, he would counter act it with peace.

Clearly, Richard had come to adhere to Proverbs 15:1, *"A gentle answer deflects anger, but harsh words make tempers flare."* I am so grateful that my husband viewed me through the lenses-of-love at that time. Proverbs 21:9, 25:24, offer husbands the following advice, *"It's better to live alone in the corner of an attic than with a quarrelsome wife in a lovely home."* I count myself fortunate that he did not detach from me, but continued to cover me with prayer. Richard gleaned such strength, wisdom, and resolve through the Holy Spirit. Like a harness, he embraced and covered me with love, joy, peace, patience, kindness, goodness, faithfulness, gentleness, and self-control (Galatians 5:22 NLT).

Listen up church folk, it is one thing to hear the Word of God, but it's another thing to respect and live it. I'm reminded of a time when Richard and I both had agreed that we would seize an opportunity, but disagreed on when would be the best timeframe to carry it out. I felt as though doing things his way would delay or deny us of great opportunities for advancement. I was convinced that I was right, and he was wrong; and I was determined to win him over to support my view.

I strategized on how I would influence my husband to do what I wanted him to do, the way I wanted him to do it, in the time frame in which I wanted it done. I was convinced that what I was about to do was okay, because my intentions were to benefit us both. Furthermore, I believed that since I was "anointed," it was God who gave me the ability to view the situation as I did. Perhaps I was being led by God to sway Richard in my favor. However, God was not having it! I clearly heard the Lord say, *"But I love him too.*" Nothing more – nothing less! In all honesty, no interpretation was needed. I understood exactly what God was saying. With strong conviction, I repented and shut that plan down without hesitation!

Romans 2:1-16 confirms that God is not a respecter of persons – period! He expects His righteous to behave, and uphold His standard in every situation. He does not love, respect, or protect one spouse, any more, or less than the other. His Word clearly states that He will judge everyone according to what he or she has done, not what he or she had *good intentions* of doing. The Word says, "*People may be pure in their own eyes, but the Lord examines their motives. Commit your actions to the Lord, and your plans will succeed*" (Proverbs 16:2-3).

Furthermore, God's reasoning for telling me, "*But I love him too,*" was to remind me that my husband, too, has the Holy Spirit living on the inside of him. So, if I intentionally or carelessly manipulate, deceive, or hurt my husband in any way, I simultaneously do the same to the Holy Spirit, and ultimately myself; because Richard and I, too, are <u>one</u>. I was not at all angry or resentful. In fact, I praised God for His correction, direction, and protection.

Although I sometimes struggled with pride, (among other issues) in the past, I really loved my husband and I wanted our marriage to work. I was also well aware of the fact that God had no problem humbling me, if I chose not to do so myself (unfortunately I've learned that the hard way in the past, a time or two). Therefore, I humbly and willfully adhered to the Word of God, and submitted to my husband.

The number one thing a man desires from a woman is honor. And I love and honor Richard very much! I have no problem expressing my respect by submitting to him as my head, and honoring his position as my "safety" (Ephesians 5:22). In fact, I take pleasure in doing so. If you are a wife, I encourage you to honor your husband as often as possible. If you are not married yet, I encourage you to take notes, study, and start applying it toward your spiritual husband (Jesus Christ) now:

"For your royal husband delights in your beauty; honor him, for he is your lord." (Psalms 45:11).

Allow God to delight in the beauty of your holiness. Allow your spiritual, as well as your physical husband to wash you with the Word of God. The Lord graciously delivered and washed me with His Word, and with that freedom came strength and joy. Furthermore, the more Richard and I submitted ourselves to God, the easier it was to submit to one another as well. It is through my husband's unwavering support, innumerable displays of compassion and forgiveness, and his intentional commitment to protect me – that is most influential to me, our family, and many others.

The following poem, entitled, "HUSBAND," is simply one way in which I choose to express how much I love and appreciate Richard, and all the sacrifices he makes *to protect and secure (me) against failure, breakage, or an accident.*"

<u>HUSBAND</u>

Husband of honor
Husband of grace
It is a blessing to be your mate.

Husband of faith
Husband of concern

From your side I will not turn.

Husband of treasures
Husband of wealth
Continue to prosper in love and good health.

Husband of protection
Husband of peace
I pray your strength will never fade or cease.

Husband of covenant
The storms of life we will weather
With God's guidance, our love, and unity,
We will overcome them together.

Husband of protection
You are the epitome of a "real" man
Never retreat from taking a righteous stand.

Husband of duty
Whether in this land or away
Never fall short to believe God and pray.

Husband of vision
I support your decision,
to follow your dreams with passion and precision.

Husband for all time,
I am your wife,
And I take pleasure to love you for the rest of my life!

CHAPTER 6

THE POWER OF AN INFLUENTIAL WOMAN

"There are many virtuous and capable women in the world, but you surpass them all!

(Proverbs 31:29 NLT)

Some years ago while \dining out, I decided to inquire about a pattern I had observed my wife develop over a period of time. I noticed she consistently preferred her drinking water with lemon. The more I observed, the more curious I became as to the benefit she gleaned from it. When I asked Renda about it, she explained that lemon is a natural cleanser and has various benefits. She went on to say lemon works well with water, and the healthy difference she believed it was making for her.

Renda's reasoning sounded sensible. Ironically though, she made no attempt to get me to adopt her "lemon-water" perspective and follow suit. There was no need to because her knowledgeable, confident, and detailed explanation not only satisfied my curiosity, but made a big impact on me as well. I too began adding lemon to my drinking water. She then began to observe my preference for lemon in my drinking water and asked, "*Honey, what made you start ordering your water with lemon*?" I replied, "*I want to be cleansed and healthier too.*"

She had not realized it, but she had managed to *influence* me without saying a word. She had effortlessly gained my submission with her consistency, confidence, and wisdom – unintentionally. I also appreciated the fact that she did not try to manipulate, deceive, or force me in any way into doing what she believed was best for me – while justifying her actions with the excuse of having "*good intentions.*" She did not try to set me up for a movie night, and slip in a "*50 reasons why lemon water is beneficial*" documentary. She did not feel the need to constantly remind me of how sick and tired she was of me not listening to her, nor did she try to beat-me-over-the-head with why I should simply follow her advice because she's a nurse (which automatically makes her right and me wrong). She allowed her considerable and influential anointing to work through her. Some of you may be thinking,

"Dude, being influenced to drink lemon-water is not a big deal." But what is a big deal for me, and probably for most, is how the process took place – without a manipulating, deceitful, and controlling attitude and agenda. Let's be real. Manipulation, deceit, and self-seeking agendas are demonic 'burglars,' pursuing every opportunity to rob countless couples of their love, trust, commitment, security, "like," favor, unity, purpose, and power. Renda and I understand all too well how the mishandling of a simple "lemon-water" observation, can quickly transition into an all-out "corned beef and cabbage" situation. We must not let our guards down, and remain vigilant in protecting our marriage from those "little foxes." Therefore, we both are grateful to God and one another for every victory, whether it be in a small battle or a sizable war.

THE POWER OF AN INFLUENTIAL WIFE

God created man (man and woman) with the power to influence; especially in marriage. Yet it is up to the husband and wife in which way each chooses to execute it – whether in a good way or in a bad way. The bible tells us that whichever way one chooses will be witnessed by everyone, and directly influence and affect one's family in some way or another. It also goes on to advise one in his or her decision making,

"Today I have given you the choice between life and death, between blessings and curses. Now I call on heaven and earth to witness the choice you make. Oh, that you would choose life, so that you and your descendants might live!" (Deuteronomy 30:19 NLT)

Early on in our marriage, there was a time in which I ignored the advice of God's Word. I made choices that literally put my marriage and life in danger of ending very badly. I hurt and disappointed my wife, family, myself, and God. I had a habit of smoking marijuana as a teenager, but thought I had control over it. I was in serious denial of how this drug actually controlled me. So much so, my addiction escalated to marijuana laced with cocaine. My self-seeking decision to descend into that slippery slope, caused me to put my life and marriage on a path to destruction. But, if it were not for the love, grace, mercy, and influential anointing of God, moving through my wife Renda (a.k.a. my 'rib') – I can assure you I would not be where I am today.

I remember one evening when I came home high as a kite and defiant. Instead of fighting with me, she chose to fight for me. She fearlessly looked me straight in the eyes, and spoke with authority to the demonic spirits oppressing me. She stated that God had given her authority over demons and not the other way around. She went on to say how I, nor our family, did not belong to satan and was not subject to any demonic spirits or curses. She also said that our home was where the Holy Spirit lived, and where the Spirit of the Lord is; there is freedom from oppression. She concluded by binding the spirits in the name of Jesus and commanding them to leave.

I tried to act as though her words meant nothing, but truthfully it scared me pretty badly and blew my high. Renda never relented from prayer, and had others praying for me as well. There were no derogatory or demeaning remarks, and no aggression. I had never experienced anything like that before, and could not wrap my head around it. It is one thing for a husband or wife to experience love, unity, and bliss with his or her spouse during the good times in a marriage. Yet it is altogether phenomenal to experience unconditional love, forgiveness, encouragement, and unwavering support from a spouse during a time of major challenges in a marriage.

I had battled the addiction off and on for about five or six months. By that time my disobedience and excuses had run their course. Some of the people who had been praying for me, were now praying for, and advising Renda to leave me. She was told that I would only drag her and the kids down with me. Renda was given the option for her and the kids to live with a family member until she could get back on her feet. She was encouraged to consider my past incarceration and battle with addiction at that time, and accept that it was **impossible** for me to change. I completely understand that those people were not telling her these things to hurt her, but to help because they loved her and our children.

My "rock bottom" opportunity to sincerely humble myself had come, when I seriously injured my hand and had to undergo surgery. I was in a lot of mental, emotional, and now physical pain as well. That was truly it for me! I felt completely helpless. I had no strength of my own and had to totally depend on God and Renda. I apologized to her for all I had put her and our family through, shared how I had surrendered my life to the Lord, and vowed that I was done with using drugs. I told her how much I loved her and the kids, and really wanted my family back. She reluctantly agreed to stay with me.

You see, most people, especially those with an addiction, often make the mistake of confusing God's patience during his or her "prodigal" experience, with acceptance or ignorance of his or her behavior. To them, when God does not allow anything drastic or life-threatening to occur in their life for a lengthy period of time, people assume they have successfully managed to hide "under the radar," and that God is not aware of what they're continuously doing. They become master manipulators and deceivers, who believe their own lies. But don't get it misconstrued! As Galatians 6:7 says, "*Be not deceived: God is not mocked: for whatsoever a man soweth, that shall ho also reap.*" I cried out to God and poured my heart out and asked Him to help me. I also vowed to never touch drugs again. That was the day in which I was truly ready to submit to God and receive His deliverance from the bondage of that addiction. I was ready and willing to transition into the man, husband, and father I was created and predestined to be.

About a week or so after my surgery, the pain engulfed my entire limb. The pain, along with my attitude, was awful. I saw myself as a victim in indescribable pain who should be comforted. I was so selfish. I had quickly forgotten all about the pain, disappointment, and shame I had caused everyone else for the last six months.

Overwhelmed, Renda had surpassed hurt and shifted to full blown anger. During a brief phone conversation one morning with a loved one, she was reminded of how foolish and ridiculous she looked to others for staying in the marriage and helping me during my post-surgical rehab and detoxing. She was strongly encouraged to get out of the marriage quickly before I relapsed. It had become apparent at that time that my wife was virtually at her wits end and ready to leave me for good. However, she shared a conversation with me that she had with God that morning that changed everything.

Renda said God told her not to leave me, so she asked, "*Lord, why should I stay? You know everything he has put us through, and how foolish I look to people. I don't want to deal with it anymore. Lord, why should I believe him? Why would this time be any different?"* The Lord then asked her, *"Are those people your God, or am I your God?"* She replied, *"Lord, You are my God."* The Lord went on to say, *"The problem isn't your believing other people, or even Richard. It is your failure to believe Me. You believe in Me, but that isn't the same as **believing Me**. You must go further and activate your faith. I want you to stay with Richard; but give him to me. If you do what I tell you to do, I promise you that I will remove the desire and appetite for drugs from his heart, and he will not touch it again. If you pay **no** attention to what others think, and do as I say; I will bless your marriage and family more than you could ever imagine."* She responded, *"Yes Lord, I will,"* as a fountain of tears streamed down her face. Renda said God then instructed her to create an atmosphere of praise by playing worship CDs over, and over, and over again; as often as possible. She was also told to encourage me, and to never use my past as leverage to attack, retaliate, or manipulate me.

It was at that moment that Renda made the decision to transition from merely believing in God to literally **believing God** without doubting, despite how foolish she appeared to others and even herself. In other words, she doubted her own doubt! Her sacrificial decision to accept and activate her role as an individual vehicle for God's purpose for my life, in conjunction with hers, annihilated generational curses and positioned our family to live victorious in every area of our lives. I can honestly say Renda has never used my past against me, even to this day. I am so fortunate to have the beautiful (inside and out), God-loving, powerful, influential woman that I have. I cannot thank her enough for her willingness to long-suffer with me, and allow God to express His unconditional love, forgiveness, mercy, grace, strength, and help through her; during that time.

YES, THAT'S MY GIRL!

Proverbs 31:29 states, *"There are many virtuous and capable women in the world, but you surpass them all!"* The full chapter describes a woman who is a beautiful and priceless treasure to her husband, her family, herself, and most importantly God. Not because of what she possesses on the outside – but because of what she possesses on the inside. She is described as moral, skilled, priceless, trustworthy, an enhancement, favored, wise, nurturing, strategic, an investor, strong, hardworking, creative, stunning, a business woman, humble, confident, articulate, compassionate, a teacher, discerning, loving, caring, highly-esteemed, beautiful, God-fearing, blessed, influential, and prestigious.

In my eyes, this describes my wife Renda perfectly. She is relentless in her pursuit to fulfill God's strategic plan for our lives, in the midst of balancing every other area. I know men who would be seriously intimidated by a wife who fits that description, but I'm not the least bit intimidated. I don't have to feel insecure or threatened by that because the plan includes us both, along one another's side.

I remember years ago when Renda was invited to minister one night, at the church we attended at the time. I was a part of the pastor's assistant's and security ministries. I, and those who served along with me, would rotate according to a prepared schedule. I had no problem serving my pastor, first lady, and other guest speakers in the past, and this service would be no different. In fact, I wanted to be sure I was on duty that night to ensure I covered my wife personally. Besides, who better to serve and cover my wife with loyalty and love (spiritually and physically) other than myself?

As I waited to escort my wife into the sanctuary, someone asked me, "*Man, it won't bother you to serve your wife as she ministers tonight, when you should be the one up there ministering?*" I replied, "*Not at all, because when my wife is up there, we both are up there; regardless of who God sends first. We are one. Therefore, we submit to one another and more importantly God. So, I have no problem waiting. And in the meantime, I have a responsibility to cover my cover my wife, and wouldn't have it any other way.*"

A husband should never be intimidated by the anointing on his wife's life because you two are one. If you are a husband with a wife who ministers God's Word, you should love and always cover her; not smother her. I absolutely love the fact that my wife is a wise, intelligent, strong, enthusiastic, strategic, anointed, influential go-getter, yet she embodies the Holy Spirit to balance her out with humility, submission, unselfishness, and love for God and me. It took those attributes to deal with many of the things my wife has gone through in her life, not to mention what I took her through in the beginning as well. So, it would not be fair for me in any way, to manipulate her into submerging certain attributes to comfort my ego and assert more control.

I praise God Renda did not 'dummy-down' for me. I was able to glean from her wisdom, strength, enthusiasm, perseverance, and influential love and obedience to Christ when I needed it most. It was my wife's consistency that really drew me to her, and more importantly – to Christ. She prayed, loved, and trusted God no differently outside of church as she did within the church. Her love and dedication to Christ was undeniable, and for me, that was intoxicating!

Truthfully, there were times in the beginning of our marriage when it irritated me to hear Renda pray as much as she did. But ironically, the more she prayed, the more enticed I became with learning how to pray and develop a "healthy" relationship with the Lord as well. What influenced me the most was that Renda did not pray for God to change me for herself. She prayed for God to change me for Christ. This is because she understood that her love for me is healthy when Christ is first, because it is Christ who first loved her – showing her what true authentic love is. In return, He shows her how to show me "healthy" unconditional love on a continuous basis, and vice-versa (1st Corinthians 7:14-16, Ephesians 5:25,33).

Some of you may be thinking, "*I wish I had a wife like that.*" Thing is, you don't have to wish for it. All women were created to walk in her influential anointing. But you, husband, have to make the decision to "man-up" and **help her develop and bring it forth**. God's Word instructs, "

"*Husbands, love your wives [seek the highest good for her and surround her with a caring, unselfish love], just as Christ also loved the church and gave Himself up for her, so that He might sanctify the church, having cleansed her by the washing of water with the word [of God],* **so that [in turn] He might present the church to himself in glorious splendor, without spot or wrinkle or any such thing; but that she would be holy [set apart for**

*God] and blameless. Even so husbands should and are morally obligated to love their own wives as [being in a sense] their own bodies. He who loves his own wife loves himself. For no one ever hated his own body, but [instead] **he nourishes and protects and cherishes it, just as Christ does the church**, because we are members (parts) of His body"* (Ephesians 5:25-30 AMP).

Therefore, when we read about the **Influential Woman of Proverbs 31**, we understand that what she possesses on the inside, is a result of what God, through her husband; helped her develop, transition, and bring forth. Her husband is in no way jealous and intimidated by her. He respects and appreciates her wisdom, and treasures her worth. In fact, he too reaps the benefits of her reputation of worthiness as stated in Proverbs 31:23, *"Her husband is well known at the city gates, where he sits with the other civic leaders."*

He understands his pinnacle power lies within their partnership with one another and God, and his ability to assist her with her purpose. He has done his job so well, that their children take notice and rise-up to honor her. He has no desire to embarrass, degrade, or discredit her. In fact, he is her greatest supporter as he publicly praises her in Proverb 31:29, *"There are many virtuous and capable women in the world, but you surpass them all!"* He views her through the lenses-of-love. He sees her as nothing less than "bone of his bone" and "flesh of his flesh." He loves his *"rib,"* his *"favor-magnet,"* and protects her as he would himself. Now that's one blessed guy to have such an awesome, influential girl! And that is why I praise God that I can truly say, *"Yes, Renda's that girl for me!"*

You may desire to experience the same with your wife and may be asking, *"Where do I start?"* You start by humbling yourself, praying for both you and your wife, and submitting yourself to God completely. Ask Him to first show you **your *"real"* self**. Receive His corrective feedback, and follow whatever instructions He gives you without deviating. Be the godly example and protector you were created to be. Ask God to strengthen and guide you to make whatever necessary changes within yourself first, instead of trying to control and correct your spouse and her issues – while justifying your own. The stronger you are, the better you can help your wife to develop, transition, and bring forth God's influential anointing within her. Also, pray with your wife and pursue godly change together. This invites God into the equation, which increases your strength, protection, effectiveness, and influential anointing within your marriage and bloodline (Ecclesiastes 4:12).

CHAPTER 7

HOW TO GET YOUR "LIKE" BACK

> "But I have this complaint against you. You don't love me or each other as you did at first!"
>
> Revelation 2:4 NLT

If we had a dollar for every time we have heard someone say, "*I love my spouse, but I'm just not 'in love' anymore*," we would probably have collected millions by now. You or someone you know may have sincerely uttered those same words and think similarly. However, it is highly likely that most of you who assume that you are no longer "*in love*" with your spouse – still are. Yet, could it be that you simply don't "***like***" your spouse anymore? Hold on before you rule it out. We want you to take a minute to listen and think.

The word **like** means:

"***to feel affection toward, take pleasure in, and enjoy being with someone.***"

Could there be a chance that you really love your spouse, yet at some point you **lost affection toward**, **don't take pleasure in**, and **don't enjoy being with** your spouse anymore?

You may have suffered an unfair share of past "trust" breaches from your spouse (infidelity, addiction issues, financial mismanagement, etc.) You may be someone who does not feel emotionally connected anymore. For you, "*the thrill is gone*" as they say! Along with that thrill, went your 'zeal' and attraction toward your spouse as well.

As a result, you may feel you are not obligated to uphold your martial or moral commitment. Furthermore, you may find yourself "*liking*" and even fantasizing about being with someone else. There may be a person or persons you enjoy fantasizing about; some of which you *think* you would like to live with. But who is that one you *know* you would not want to live without?

Consider the following:

1. What were the **two** things you were most attracted to when you two first started dating?

Choose from the following: physical appearance, intellect, spiritual faith, personality, credit score, occupation, goals, age, financial portfolio, determination?

2. What were the **two** things you were least attracted to when you two first started dating? Choose from the following: physical appearance, intellect, spiritual faith, personality, credit score, occupation, goals, age, financial portfolio, determination?

3. In the beginning, what was it that really connected you two?

4. When did you know that you wanted to marry your spouse?

5. Which of the following was your decision to marry your spouse based on?

   o The way he or she made you feel whenever you two were with one another?

   o You could not stop thinking about him or her whenever you two were apart?

6. Lastly, we want you to locate that **one** thing that made you realize that although you had over seven billion people on this earth to

choose from, you specifically chose your spouse as the one person you did not want to spend the rest of your life *without*.

Now for the next sixty seconds, meditate on how that **one** thing has been pivotal in changing the trajectory of your life for the better.

BACK TO THE BASICS

It is time to evaluate your current situation. If your relationship was a blazing flame, but now it barely flickers; you will need to go back-to-the-basics and reevaluate what first ignited your flame. To accurately do so, you can begin by answering the following:

1. Is that **one** thing that made my spouse irresistible to me when we first started dating still visible, tangible, and accessible to me today? If not, why?
2. Is that **one** thing that made me irresistible to my spouse when we first started dating still visible, tangible, and accessible to my spouse today? If not, why?

3. What is my spouse's favorite food, gift, or place to visit? Has it changed since we first married? How do I know? When was the last time my spouse and I discussed my spouse's favorite things?

4. What is my favorite food, gift, and place to visit? Has it changed since we first married? If so, does my spouse know? When is the last time my spouse and I discussed my favorite things?

5. When was the last <u>random</u> (without being prompted) act of appreciation I expressed toward my spouse? How well was it received by my spouse?

6. When was the last <u>random</u> (without being prompted) act of appreciation my spouse expressed toward me? How well was it received by me?

After completing the exercise:

1. Exchange answers.

2. Discuss your answers in a humble and considerate manner.

3. Encourage and comfort one another.

4. Together, write out a plan for corrections and updates.
5. Take prompt action to implement.
6. Repeat exercise every 3-6 months.

We believe "*Back-to-the-Basics*" is essential. Its humbling, team approach has proven successful for our own marriage as well. We each have that one thing that proved to be the hook-in-the-jaw that we happily surrendered to, and remains pivotal in fusing us together:

> ➤ Richard – "*It was Renda's genuine and relentless love for God that sealed the deal for me.*"
> ➤ Renda – "*It was Richard's unwavering confidence that always made me feel safe.*"

This strategic exercise can be very useful. It not only raises awareness, but offers hope and encouragement. It gives couples a starting point to recapture their "like," re-awaken their love, and reinforce their commitment for their relationship and marriage. It also gives couples the foresight of how to wisely proceed when it comes to making any necessary adjustments.

The strategies we present to you work no different for us. We too must choose to stand together and continue to discuss and reevaluate our relationship's strengths and frailties, as well as our own individual issues. We must continually remain unified spiritually and physically. Unification (with husband, wife, and God) is the critical key to strategically increasing and executing the maximum strength needed for conquering a variety of challenges as stated in Ecclesiastes 4:9-12, "*Two people are better off than one, for they can help each other succeed. If one person falls, the other can reach out to help. But someone who falls alone is in real trouble. Likewise, two people lying close together can keep each other warm. But how can one be warm alone? A person standing alone can be attacked and defeated, but two can stand back-to-back and conquer. Three are even better, for a triple-braided cord is not easily broken.*"

HOW TO HANDLE YOUR 'DIS'LIKES & 'DIS'AGREEMENTS

Couples are constantly evolving as a team, as well as individuals. So, it should not come as a surprise that you and your spouse's thoughts, opinions, interest, experiences, and most of all your "*likes*" may appear to differ greatly at times. But no matter how uncomfortable, vulnerable, or sensitive an atmosphere of disagreement may become, it is not the time for you to alienate yourself or leave your spouse – especially angrily. Instead, it is at this time that you draw closer to your spouse by humbling yourself, praying with him or her, and seeking God's guidance together. Ephesians 4:26-27, 31-32 NLT advises, "*And 'Don't sin by letting anger control you.' Don't let the sun go down while you are still angry, for anger gives a foothold to the devil. (31) Get rid of all bitterness, rage, anger, harsh words, and slander, as well as all types of evil behavior. Instead, be kind to each other, tenderhearted, forgiving one another, just as God through Christ has forgiven you.*" In return, you two can 'agree-to-disagree' with one another, yet allow God's Word to "steer-the-ship" of your relationship and draw you two closer to Him, as well as one another.

WEIGHT

Honestly, weight has been a topic of discussion for us periodically as well. In times past, just the thought of talking about it brought on feelings of anxiety, apprehension, and even fear of a misunderstanding or major blow-up. Fortunately, the discussion of weight, and how to best deal with it isn't an issue we get upset about, or 'tip-toe' around anymore. We now understand that we can avoid very sensitive, and a potentially hostile subject from escalating into an all-out hurtful war of words that divides and conquers us.

Understand, there's nothing wrong with spouses being open and honest with one another when it comes to corrective criticism and healthy lifestyle changes. Especially regarding weight. Although important, these topics can be highly sensitive and emotionally draining. Therefore, both spouse's privacy should be considered and respected. It is vital that the topic is approached and discussed in a humble and considerate manner as well.

When it comes to us discussing one another's weight, it is important to us that we both are comfortable, considerate, respectful, and more importantly – realistic! We say this because many people tend to expect his or her spouse's metabolism to work just as efficiently and quickly at forty-five as it did at twenty-five. Let's just be honest. For most people, that is unrealistic. So, formulate a strategic weight loss or healthier lifestyle plan that will work for each of you; and work together. Encourage and support each other along your journey no matter what. Remember, there is no "I" in team…and its teamwork that makes the dream work! For us, we choose to keep in mind that it may have been our spouse's outer beauty that captured our eyes, but it was the inner beauty that captured our heart.

QUENCHING OUR THIRST

Have you ever experienced being so thirsty that you drank a liquid of some sort, other than water, but it could not quench your thirst? It did not matter that its ingredients contained a percentage of water, or its label read "artificial flavored water" – it simply could not get the job done. It was unable to quench your thirst because it simply was not one hundred percent, authentic water. It does not matter whether it's spring, distilled, or purified from a faucet or a bottle – as long as it is genuine water. Nothing, and I mean absolutely no other beverage in this world is greater than, or equal to water. Therefore, nothing artificial or any other substitute will suffice. The fact is – water is unequivocally **irreplaceable**! We choose to intentionally view one another, and our marriage no differently than water – *irreplaceable*. We encourage you to do the same – for good reason.

Case-in-point # 4:

.

Richard's "Barrel" Revelation

Many years ago, there was a time when Renda and I went through quite a bit of turmoil in our relationship. It was obvious that we could not see eye-to-eye on much of anything. Our frequent arguments and disagreements were deafening. I admit about ninety-percent of it was my fault. During that time, I would unleash a slew of verbal put-downs, complaints, and insults toward Renda. I was notorious for taking her weaknesses and struggles, magnifying them, and using them against her whenever we argued. Ironically, she never used my past incarceration or battle with drugs against – no matter how deeply I may have verbally and emotionally wounded her. But that was not the case for me. Although I never physically abused her in any way – my mouth was verbally lethal.

I could not see the full extent of how negatively effective my actions were, until one of our daughters (who was very young at the time) expressed to us that she did not **ever** want to get married. Somewhat shocked, we probed her as to why she felt that way. She went on to explain that she did not think marriage was for her, because she could **never** stand for her husband to talk to her the way in which I talked to my wife. I tell you, that pretty much hit me right between the eyes! Shortly after, I caught a fraction of a pastor's sermon on TV, which included an analogy that was similar to the following (I would like to give him credit, but I honestly don't know who he was):

Both spouses come into their marriage with two barrels for one another to consistently drink from. One barrel is strong and full, and the other is weak and empty. The full barrel represents the "godly" qualities, strengths, and nutrients your spouse utilizes to bless you and your relationship. The empty, weak barrel represents your negative complaints about your spouse's weaknesses. Daily you are given a choice to draw from either of the two barrels for nourishment, and to "quench your thirst." The wise choice would be for you two to draw from one another's full, strong barrel. In return, you both will be strengthened to assist one another with the weak, empty barrel.

That was literally life-changing for me! I immediately repented to God, and asked for His forgiveness and help. I apologized to my wife and family for my rude and hurtful behavior. From that moment on, I made it my mission to be the man, husband, father, and godly example I was created and instructed to be. I would speak blessings; not curses. I would lift-up, and not tear down. I stopped attacking my wife with her weaknesses, and began to help her gain victory over them. My decision to draw

DON'T DIVORCE OVER CORNED BEEF & CABBAGE

from Renda's 'full' barrel consistently, helped to restore our lenses-of-love, which strengthened and encouraged us both.

We have six daughters. I did not want to be the reason any one of them, or any of my children, would deliberately choose to forfeit the blessing of marriage due to roots of fear, anger, bitterness, resentment, or unforgiveness that I provoked. God's word clearly warns **us fathers**,

> ➢ "Fathers, provoke not your children to anger, lest they be discouraged." (Colossians 3:21)
> ➢ "And, ye fathers, provoke not your children to wrath: but bring them up in the nurture and admonition of the Lord." (Ephesians 6:4)

I want all of our children, and our children's children, to be able to engage in healthy relationships and 'grow' forward. Renda and I both are committed to maintaining God's marital standard, by choosing to humble ourselves and balance our battles wisely – together!

Our choice to draw from one another's "full" barrel instead of the "empty" barrel, helped to transform our distorted view of one another, and our marriage. Although the wise choice may seem obvious, many couples choose otherwise. We were fortunate. Despite facing some serious hurdles, we remained committed to our marriage and one another. We both are grateful to God and one another that we made the right choice.

We knew that had we chose to divorce one another, there would be a chance that we each could find someone new, and remarry. In addition, we also understood that there was a chance for us each to meet someone quite similar in physical appearance, temperament, personality, or even financial success – but we weren't fools! We also clearly understood the risks we would be taking. Not only would a new spouse not be able to provide the previous spouse's "*unique*," strong, full barrel content (which drew us to fall in love with one another to begin with); yet he or she would also come into the relationship with a whole new **weak**, "empty" barrel for us to accept as well.

Our greatest divorce deterrent is that although our "*like*" managed to get buried deep within that weak, empty barrel of complaints at one time; we still deeply love one another. In addition, we are committed to our covenant. And although we have experienced some turbulent ups-and-downs during the last two decades, neither one of us wants to live without one another's barrels. We know how important and maritally lucrative it is for us to be transparent and realistic with ourselves and one another. In our pursuit to obtain God's wisdom regarding marriage, we've also obtained the understanding of the following two principles:

R & R's Marriage Principle #1

To marry, receive, and enjoy my spouse's strong, "full" barrel, is to also marry, accept, and <u>assist</u> <u>my</u> <u>spouse</u> with his or her weak, "empty" barrel as well.

R & R's Marriage Principle #2

*"What one views as **irreplaceable**, one will treasure."*

These principles are now sewn into the fabric of our marital foundation, and serves as a continuous lifeline in our marriage. As a result, it drastically decreases the vulnerability and probability of our "*like*" being hijacked. **We believe there would be a substantial decrease in divorces if couples would agree to** view one another as *"irreplaceable,"* and redirect their attention to repairing their *"like,"* and refrain from abandoning their "love."

CHAPTER 8

BECOMING A POWER PAIR

> *"Can two people walk together without agreeing on the direction?"*
>
> *(Amos 3:3 NLT)*

God created the first **Power Pair** – Adam and Eve. You may be thinking, *"What exactly is a Power Pair?"* The word *"power"* means *"control or influence,"* and the word *"pair"* is defined as *"two things that are the same and are meant to be used together."* Put the two together and you have ***an influential couple who agree, and purposely work together in unison with one another and God; to impact the world***. This reflects God's Strategic Blueprint for Marriage.

God creates, develops, and instructs married couples to become a Power Pair. He influences them through His Word and Spirit, and in return, they are empowered to influence others. Therefore, Power Pairs must respect and adhere to God's blueprint standard, to ensure fulfillment of their marital purpose. It would be great if every married couple set their marital foundation and standard according to God's Strategic Blueprint for marriage, but unfortunately that is not the case. In fact, statistics show the following:

> ➢ In America, there is one divorce approximately every 36 seconds. That's nearly 2,400 divorces per day, 16,800 divorces per week and 876,000 divorces a year. (Washington Divorce & Family Lawyer, 2017)

The enemy uses the same strategy of **visual detachment** against marriages in this present day, just as he did on the very first marriage. His ultimate goal is to influence and lead as many married couples to divorce as possible. He wants to derail spouses from fulfilling their God-given purpose as **one** unit or team. Unfortunately, many have fallen prey to his plan, but you two, don't have to.

Purpose is to a marriage, what vision is to a man – a lifeline, *"Where there is no vision [revelation of God and his word], the people are unrestrained; But happy and blessed is he who keeps the law [of God]."* (Proverbs 29:18 AMP). It is like wind to a sail – It helps you to keep ***pressing*** toward the vision. Every married couple should know God's purpose for their marriage, and erect a marital vision and strategy for its success. Truth is, real marital success is not about fulfilling unrealistic expectations you, your spouse, and others may envision for your marriage. Real marital success is about fulfilling the purpose God predestined for your marriage. Do you know the purpose for your marriage? What is your marital vision? If you do not already know your marital purpose, or have a vision established, now is the time to seek out, create, and cultivate them together.

There are many spouses who say they are desperate for change concerning their marriage. There are those who pray for God to reposition them into His purpose and plan for their lives, as quickly as possible. Yet, sometimes the only thing that stands between experiencing life as usual, and experiencing marriage at its best – is motion failure. To make the decision to change is only the beginning. It is when you put your faith in action that the deal is sealed. If one truly desires marital transformation, one must execute one hundred percent faith activation – and "grow" for it – together!

"GROW" FOR IT!

A couple's willful, spiritual growth and maturity are essential nutrients for inserting change. It begins with faith. Although Mark 9:23 tells us that faith makes all things possible, understand that it takes "work" to help them manifest:

"Now someone may argue, "Some people have faith; others have good deeds." But I say, "How can you show me your faith if you don't have good deeds? I will show you my faith by my good deeds" (James 2:18 NLT). Therefore, as James 2:20 states, faith, without its activation, is useless. It would be equivalent to hoping for a gift card, receiving it, but never using it.

Honestly, some people have simply adapted to a faithless atmosphere. They have submitted to a complacent, pacified, fearful, pessimistic, or downright lazy lifestyle, and choose not to "grow" for the marriage they claim to desire. In the meantime, they no longer desire God, or their spouse anymore. This is usually a result of a lack of prayer, fasting, intimacy, and reading the Word of God – together.

All too often we here husbands and wives go on-and-on about how much they love their spouses, and desire to save their marriage – but reject the very thought of sacrificing and long-suffering with their spouse.

Many couples say they love one another, yet some *"fruit"* or evidence show otherwise. John 3:16 NLT says, *"For this is how **God loved** the world: **He gave** his one and only **Son,** so that everyone who believes in him will not perish but have eternal life."* Christ **gave up His life** for the church, and you have church folk who refuse to "push-back-a-plate" for their spouse! Christ has been **very** patient with His bride for thousands of years, and you have folks who can't stand to show compassion toward their spouse for two hours! Christ paid-it-all for the church, and you have folks who complain about paying a cell phone bill for their spouse who legitimately needs their help. Christ did it all for his bride **without complaining,** because **He really loves her**! Instead of using the Church's weaknesses against her, **Christ supported her with His strength**. And **together**, they continue to change the world!

So, we ask you; *are you really loving your spouse, right*? Christ stated in Revelation 2:4 NLT, *"But I have this complaint against you. You don't love me or each other as you did at first!"* If this charge was made against you today, would your current treatment toward your spouse acquit or convict you?

Countless life-changing opportunities have been forfeited due to what we call the "settler syndrome." These are the people who have chosen to settle for far less than what was "possible" for them. They tend to be unfulfilled, "consistent" complainers. They are dissatisfied with where they are in life, but are not willing to take the necessary steps to grow-forward and shift from pacified to satisfied. They often unintentionally discourage others, by way of a negative outlook toward anything that requires one to operate in faith – supported by works. Although, a number of couples may know *"all things are possible with God,"* according to Matthew 19:26, they often choose to doubt God's Word. They publicly express to others their belief *in* God, while privately they struggle to simply ***believe*** Him. This can open the door to confusion.

We, in our human nature, have a tendency to render a firm reprimand to others, when we should graciously correct; and we graciously correct during a time that calls for a firm reprimand. This confusion can result in a debilitating detour from the correct course of action for a couple's growth and development, resulting in an eclipse of their purpose. Therefore, sensitivity to the Holy Spirit is vital and literally the lifeline of a great marriage.

For example, one spouse expresses suppressive behavior toward his or her mate, because he or she blames the mate for most, or all his or her trials, setbacks, and feelings of stagnation. When in fact, the trials, setbacks, and feelings of stagnation are directly related to a lack of humility, and submission. As a result, one spouse furthers his or her own anguish, by suppressing the partner who was positioned by God to help keep him or her from falling. Basically, as he or she continues in the suppressive behavior, he or she is unknowingly "burying their blessing," resulting in the negation of possibility, forfeiture of opportunity, and the burden of regrets.

Possibility and opportunity go hand-in-hand as Ecclesiastes 9:11 tells us, *"I have observed something else under the sun. The fastest runner doesn't always win the race, and the strongest warrior doesn't always win the battle. The wise sometimes go hungry, and the skillful are not necessarily wealthy. And those who are educated don't always lead successful lives. It is all decided by chance, by being in the right place at the right time"* (NLT). Hebrews 11:1 begins, "Now faith is." *Now* is the time to "grow" for it together under the Holy Spirit's guidance. Seize any, and every opportunity God sends to knock at the door of your heart. No matter what comes your way, proceed together in unity, strategy, prayer, faith, strength, and irreplaceable love for one another.

INTIMACY

Intimacy is the main area in which couples seem to visually detach the quickest and most frequent. For starters, many are under the misconception that intimacy only refers to physical intercourse. Nothing could be further from the truth. It's cool if intimacy with your spouse leads to your bedroom, but it should never begin there. The foundation for a couple's physical intimacy with one another should be established through each spouse's spiritual intimacy with God.

What is intimacy?

> The state of being familiar; familiarity;
> To come to know; recognize
> Hebrew: (yama) – meaning "*know*"
> Greek: (ginosko) – meaning "*know*" and (koinonia) – meaning "*communion, joint participation.*"

What sets the foundation for intimacy?

> The willful presence or attendance of the participants.

What six "rights" are needed for a successful intimate exchange?

> The right partner (God, spouse)
> The right atmosphere (private)

> ➤ The right information (the team's goal)
> ➤ The right approach (best course of action)
> ➤ The right response (team's feedback / approval <u>or</u> redirection)
> ➤ The right results (**team** satisfaction)

Yes, you want the right partner, in the right atmosphere, with the right information, to determine the right approach, to get the right response, and achieve the right results. Believe it or not, the bible reveals quite a bit on the subject. If couples would take the time to actually study spiritual intimacy together, and not quickly read over, or avoid the subject altogether – we believe countless marriages could be transformed.

Consecrate yourself to God, and develop spiritual and physical discipline. It empowers you to stay submitted to God, resist sexual immorality, and walk in victory over sin; regardless of how expensive or beautifully its packaged. The foundation for a man's and woman's physical intimacy with his or her spouse, should be birthed from his or her spiritual intimacy with God. He or she should establish a consecrated covenant and *spiritual* intercourse (the act of becoming one in the spirit) with the Lord, prior to entering holy matrimony and *sexual* intercourse (the act of becoming one in the flesh) with his or her spouse. The following scripture, Song of Solomon 2:16, indicates such a covenant, *"My lover is mine, and I am his."* You can experience spiritual intimacy through a willful, one-on-one, cultivated, interactive, relationship with God. In return, you learn how to approach, duplicate, and apply it physically with your spouse.

There are various ways to ignite intimacy. One way being a captivating *aroma*. In the bible, God required an aroma (scent or smell) of "sacrifice." It was proven to be a highly successful way for man to ignite spiritual intimacy with God.

RENDA'S INTIMATE SNAPSHOT

Here is a glimpse of my intimate interchange with my first love…my ADONAI (Lord), through a poem I wrote to God many years ago:

Aroma!

Ooh, my heart cries, "Fill me!"
As your compassionate words, still me.

Just a hint of your cologne,
Let's me know I'm not alone.

Your love is evident
in my element.

Yes, your essence
has become so prevalent.

Your beauty I cannot ignore,
as my heart yearns for more.

The aroma of your fragrance is the key.
As I inhale, and capture your smell,

It unlocks my soul, and I am free.
Liberated to pursue You… my Love, my Lord— my
Destiny!

Copyright © 2005, Renda Horne

What works for God, can also work for man.
When it comes to spouses initiating physical intimacy
with one another, an "aroma" can be very intoxicating!
Let's take for instance the heavily influential perfume

and cologne business. It is a multi-billion-dollar industry for good reason – its proven effectiveness!

Again, what works for God, can also work for man. Sacrifice can be a very attractive and effective "aphrodisiac" among couples. Knowing your spouse willingly sacrificed for you, shows his or her love for you, and should provoke you to want to do *more* for him or her. In fact, Jesus told us that it is more blessed to give than to receive (Acts 20:35 NLT). Intimacy, like marriage, is teamwork and should be viewed as such. Don't assume your spouse is intimately "satisfied," because you are. He or she may only be pacified. Selfish intimacy (even if unintentional) is emotionally unhealthy, and downright toxic for any marriage. Be sure to selflessly inquire of one another, communicate effectively, and proceed accordingly (within reason of course)! Don't minimize your spouse's concerns with condescending remarks, or sarcastic undertones. Keep in mind that intimacy <u>always</u> matters in a marriage – especially to the Lord. So, stay attentive!

Great intimacy within a marriage is possible, but it does not manifest by accident. Your participation must be mutual, intentional, and fully active. You must use wisdom to formulate a good strategy, and be willing to do the work. As a couple, take the opportunity to learn and understand your marital purpose, erect a vision, and walk in your influential anointing – together. Most of all, don't allow *visual detachment* of any kind, separate you two, from the love of God, or one another.

RENDA'S RESOLUTIONN

Many of you have a misconstrued view of the role in which your spouse is obligated to play when it comes to your happiness. This was a repetitive obstacle for me early on in our marriage until God gave me the revelation that changed the course of my marriage for good. The Lord told me that I was mistreating my husband, by putting unnecessary weight and pressure on him to supply my happiness. Only God Himself can do that. He went on to say:

"*When it comes to happiness, I am the supplier and your husband is the supporter. **Happiness is a (blessed, empowered to prosper) lifestyle**, not a fluctuating feeling that shifts, according to your* *atmosphere. That's why Richard is only capable of supporting, what only I can supply."*

Wow…did you get that? Our spouses support our happiness, but only God can supply it according to Philippians 4:19. Whatever you deposit into your marriage, is what you will ultimately receive. If you understood the pivotal role in which you and your spouse play, in one another's life, it would completely change your perspective. We believe it would cause you to view your spouse and your marriage differently.

Wouldn't you like to see your spouse the way God sees him or her? Furthermore, think about the fact that satan views your and your spouse's unity in Christ, as a major threat to his agenda. Together, you are considered double-trouble. You need to understand that satan attacks your marriage based on your God-given potential, and not your present condition.

God has called you both to be great and effective leaders for others. And being a great and effective leader is not about having a title, or salivating over how much power you have over others. It is about having the wisdom to balance, and execute, love and unity, with compassion and correction, without lowering your standards or compromising your integrity.

We can honestly say that we are totally fulfilled in our marriage, and lack nothing. This is because God has given us the wisdom to know and understand the authentic ingredients for what a "*fulfilled*" marriage entails. This includes six ways to "**divorce-proof**" your marriage:

- Walk in Unconditional love
- Walk in Unconditional respect
- Walk in Unconditional support
- Walk in Unconditional honor
- Walk in Unconditional unification
- Walk in in Unconditional humility

If you could only see how great your marriage and family could be, you would simply let go of fighting with your spouse, and relentlessly fight for your spouse. The devil would no longer view you as a "chump," but FEAR you as a "CHAMP!" So, both of you remember: as the saying goes – there is no "I" in team. It will take your unified "teamwork," to make your marriage and "dream work!"

56985658R00076

Made in the USA
Columbia, SC
03 May 2019